S0-BVX-889

focus on
CANADA

◆ *inspiring places, beautiful spaces* ◆

Written by Mike Gerrard
Designed by Jeremy Tilston of The Oak Studio Limited
Produced by AA Publishing
Text © Automobile Association Developments Limited 2007
For details of photograph copyrights see page 96

All rights reserved. No part of this publication may be
reproduced, stored in a retrieval system, or transmitted in any
form or by any means – electronic, photocopying, recording
or otherwise – unless the written permission of the publisher
has been obtained beforehand.

Published by AA Publishing (a trading name of Automobile
Association Developments Limited, whose registered office
is Fanum House, Basing View, Basingstoke, Hampshire
RG21 4EA; registered number 1878835).

A03202

ISBN-10: 0-7495-5206-9
ISBN-13: 978-0-7495-5206-0

A CIP catalogue record for this book is available
from the British Library.

Colour reproduction by KDP, Kingsclere, England
Printed in China by C&C Offset Printing

PICTURES FROM TOP TO BOTTOM:
The natural beauty of Charlevoix continues off-shore in the
grassy banks of Baie-St-Paul harbor.

Canada Place, alongside Vancouver's downtown buildings, has
become a friendly face in a sometimes stark cityscape.

The melting ice of the Kaskawulsh Glacier is enough to feed
Kluane Lake, the largest lake in the Yukon.

PAGE 3: More than 200 pairs of Canada Geese nest on
Regina's Wascana Park every spring.

PAGE 4: The perfectly still waters of Hector Lake are
surrounded by the peaks of the Canadian Rockies.

focus on
CANADA
◆ *inspiring places, beautiful spaces* ◆

INTRODUCTION

Canada is the largest country in the western world: only Russia beats it on size. So rugged is some of its northern terrain that much of it remains unconquered. Heroic tales of travelers arriving in Hudson Bay or crossing the harsh Yukon in search of gold are not so far in the past. Look at some of the photographs in this book, and it could have happened last week. And yet within this massive land mass there are only six cities that have a population of more than a million. These cities all rose from a land that was inhabited originally by the people of the First Nations. Later the French came, then the British, and then came a proud independence.

These are the handful of basic elements whose wonderfully vibrant mix is shown on the following pages. First was the land. Look at the glaciers, the mountains, the rivers, and lakes. It is not a tamed land. It's a land against which man has to continue to fight, even today, to find shelter and to feed his family. From the frontier lands of the Yukon and the western seaboard, across the Canadian Rockies and the great plains, past lakes and waterfalls to the jagged fjords and fishing grounds of the eastern coast, Canada is a country of superlatives. It is also a country of individuals. A unique land like this forges a unique people. It creates pioneers, rebels, people with a distinctive point of view. It creates people who can live with the land, admire it, and respect it.

Traveling across the land, even if only in photographs, reminds us of the great people who were drawn to Canada in the past, to try to fathom its mysteries and to see if there were even more glorious sights beyond the next mountain, around the next river bend. And frequently there were. Names like John Cabot recur. The John Cabot Trail, which winds around Cape Breton Island, is hailed as one of the most beautiful motor routes in the world, a fitting way of honoring the acclaimed Italian explorer.

Despite its vast size (some 3,849,653 square miles), Canada only has two borders—with the United States and with the sea. With the one it has a mostly friendly and sometimes sharp rivalry. With the other it has fought an often life-and-death struggle for a few thousand years. The fishermen of Newfoundland and Nova Scotia, whose lives and landscapes feature so prominently in these pages, continue to battle the elements to bring back vital foods to a home where the seasons can be too short to grow land crops successfully. In the west, in places like the Pacific Rim National Park on Vancouver Island, the sea is embraced in man's protection as he tries to conserve the oceans and the forests for all our descendants.

Exactly 19,550 feet above the seas, the peak of Mount Logan in the Yukon marks the country's highest point. It stands in the Kluane National Park, whose ever-changing landscapes appear in this book. So too do those of Canada's other glorious National Parks, such as Jasper, Gros Morne, Mont Tremblant, Fundy, Forillon, Banff, and Cape Breton Islands. These protected areas are being added to all the time, for the Canadians are certainly aware of the beautiful land in which they live.

Canadians appreciate their great cities too. On the west coast, Vancouver is a Manhattan striding the Fraser River Estuary and regularly receiving some of the best 'quality of life' ratings in the world. Over in the east, Québec and Montréal add their spices to the mix. Québec is unique, a good-time Gallic city slapped down on the North American continent. Yet Montréal is the capital of French-speaking Canada, and the country's second-largest city, with a smooth mix of fine modern buildings and historical quarters, of an old port, an Olympic stadium and a cathedral called Nôtre-Dame. The nation's largest city is Toronto, and lest anyone be in any doubt about Canada's standing in the world, take one look at the CN Tower. You could hardly ask for a finer symbol for a city and a country, than the world's tallest building.

In between these superlatives, these extremes, quieter lives are being led that also build a picture of a nation: the monks in their quiet retreat at St-Benoît-du-Lac, the countryside's old barns fixed into the landscape, the Canada geese, and the carpets of wild spring flowers. A picture starts to emerge of this country, a mosaic, a tapestry. And when you look at a part, you can still see the whole for you can find Canada in the weathered color of a simple lobster pot or in the icy expanse of a glacier.

The Stewart Museum in Montréal has an impressive model of the city as it was in 1760. These soldiers carrying arms and bearing authentic uniforms bring the past even more vividly to life.
Opposite: Vancouver's 4,101-foot Grouse Mountain dwarfs the Skyride gondola, taking visitors to the top. Wild flowers carpet the lower slopes in glorious colors every spring.
Pages 6–7: Lunenburg was founded in 1753 and is now a UNESCO World Heritage Site. Its Fisheries Museum of the Atlantic celebrates the town's maritime traditions.

Toronto's CN Tower celebrated its 30th birthday on 26 June 2006. Each year more than 2 million people take the elevator ride to the top of the tallest free-standing structure in the world, all 1,815 feet and 5 inches of it.

Opposite: Halifax in Nova Scotia sits on the second largest natural harbor in the world, after Sydney in Australia. This waterfront has been a hive of shipping activity since the mid-18th century.

In Quebec's St-Benoît-du-Lac, the Abbey looks through the mist on the lake as if through the mists of time. Founded in 1912, more than fifty monks still live there in beautiful seclusion.
Opposite: on Canada's eastern seaboard, the fishermen in small communities like North Harbor enjoy a spell tied up in shelter, yet know their work will always take them back to the sea.

*Vancouver's Stanley Park incorporates activities from modern
rollerblading to the ancient traditions of the First Nations people.
The Brockton totem pole area is one of the most visited attractions
in British Columbia.*

*Opposite: the Saguenay Fjord is one of the most dramatic sights
in northern Québec. The Baie Éternité could not have been more
appropriately named.*

*Pages 14–15: in the autumnal gold of Cape Breton Island hides the
Cabot Trail. One of the most scenic drives in the world, it runs for
almost 186 miles along coast and through mountains and forest.*

The name of Pyramid Lake echoes the shapes of some of the mountains that surround it. It's set in Jasper National Park, the largest national park in the Canadian Rockies, where grizzlies, moose, wolves, and caribou roam.

On the Charlevoix coast on the north shore of the St Lawrence River, this farmer's barn seems as old as the land itself. Not quite, though, as the mountains here were formed when a meteorite hit the earth some 350 million years ago.

The Legislative Building in Regina, the capital city of Saskatchewan, watches the sun set over Wascana Lake for another day. The 174ft-high building was opened in 1912 after four years of work.
Opposite: in the Algonquin Provincial Park, Ontario's oldest, is the Barron Canyon. Formed 10,000 years ago by the force of the river, the area is home to bears, wolves and deer, along with 272 species of birds…and 1,000 types of insect.
Pages 20–21: the sun sets over Bonne Bay in western Newfoundland's Gros Morne National Park. The Maritime Archaic Indians who first settled this land 5,000 years ago would have gazed upon this very same sight.

*The rewards of early morning on Route 172 in northern Québec include the sight of mists in the trees.
Journey's end may be the pristine Baie-Sainte-Marguerite, a branch of the Saguenay Fjord.
Opposite: only 15 minutes from Vieux-Québec is the Île d'Orléans, where manor houses date back to the
18th century. One of the finest is this, the Manoir Mauvide-Genest from 1734, now a museum.
Pages 24–25: it takes nerves of steel to ride in the external glass-fronted elevators up Toronto's CN Tower.
Your reward is fine dining and views of up to 100 miles.*

On the very edge of the New World, the lights of Newfoundland's capital, St John's, shine like beacons.
For mariners and fishermen braving the North Atlantic, the Inner Harbour was a haven.

The Murray River on Prince Edward Island shelters fishing boats in its mirror-still waters. Sail out to its offshore islands, and you can find hundreds of seals basking on the rocks.
Opposite: American lobsters live off the eastern seaboard of Canada and the United States, from South Carolina all the way up to here in Newfoundland where lobster pots are stacked away outside of the fishing season.
Pages 30–31: one hour north of Montréal are the mighty Laurentian Mountains. Here there are forests, lakes, rivers and an abundance of wildlife, including moose, timber wolves and these Virginia Deer.

Mont Tremblant National Park is the largest in Québec. It is large enough to accommodate those looking for outdoor activities, while hiding quiet spots like Lac aux Rats.

The Long Point Twillingate Lighthouse in Newfoundland was built in 1875. The extent to which it is needed can be told by the fact that it sits on a place named Devil's Cove Head in Iceberg Alley.

The 226ft-tall twin towers of the Basilique Nôtre-Dame are landmarks of old Montréal. The 19th-century
interior is gloriously lit by three huge rose windows.
Opposite: at Tofino Hot Springs on Vancouver Island, a Bald Eagle sits and watches visitors come and go.
This is his home, which he shares with the Nuu-chah-nulth First Nations people.

Some of Vancouver's best restaurants are on Granville Island. With fresh ingredients like these raspberries available at the regular Monday market, that isn't surprising. Opposite: many have called Cape Breton Island the most beautiful island in the world. Here the simple manmade beauty of a traditional home complements the natural beauty of a wild meadow.

Clayoquot Sound covers 350,000 hectares of land and ocean off Vancouver Island, and is home to just five communities. Its rare temperate rainforest is a vital resource.
Opposite: the Geodesic Dome, built for Canada's Expo '86, houses the city's Science World. It attracts almost 700,000 visitors every year, and pleases even more when it's lit up at night.

Montréal is noted for the contrast between its historic and its strikingly modern buildings. This pair of
19th-century townhouses are as bright and eye-catching as anything from the 21st century.
Opposite: Fundy National Park has some of the last remaining wilderness in southern New Brunswick.
A hiking trail leads past the Dickson Falls, one of several spectacular falls in the park.

Five million people live in the Greater Toronto area, with half of those people born outside Canada. Downtown Toronto is the country's main financial and entertainment district, and beneath the skyscrapers the city continues underground.

Opposite: Canada's old barns are falling into disuse and disrepair, even being dismantled to make way for new buildings. They have been part of the landscape for 200 years, and are known as Canada's castles and cathedrals.

Pages 44–45: the Forillon National Park covers the Gaspé peninsula and has dramatic scenery where land meets sea. Cap Bon-Ami glows gold as the sun goes down.

The scenic routes around Saguenay Fjord continually demand that you stop and admire the landscape's natural wonders. This timeless spot is on Route 172, near Baie-Sainte-Marguerite. Opposite: Kluane National Park is one of Canada's great jewels. In addition to Mount Logan, the country's highest peak at 19,545ft, much of the land is covered by glaciers.

Nets and floats cram the decks of the *Atlantic Challenger*, as it waits
to brave the seas off St John's. Men have fished these Newfoundland
waters for as long as they have lived here.

Opposite: yachts cluster for shelter in the Toronto Islands, like a herd
of nervous creatures hiding from predators. Yet they are so close to
Toronto that they can be viewed from the heights of the CN Tower.

The waters of Nova Scotia are popular for whale-watching, with humpbacks, fin whales, pilot whales, minke whales and others beneath the waves—and occasionally delighting watchers with their immense leaps. Opposite: walking in the Tablelands of the Gros Morne National Park on the Island of Newfoundland brings hikers to river bridges like this—but not until July, to allow the land to recover from the winter snows.

The Old Cabbagetown quarter of Toronto is known for its Victorian
homes, its cottages, and its quirky nature. Its narrow streets hide
cottages, and the trees here almost hide this red-brick home.
Opposite: down by the harbor, Downtown Vancouver's skyscrapers
seem dwarfed by the masts. And as the evening falls, the worktown
becomes a playground.

These delicate, colorful heads of wild wheat are growing in the Yukon. The harsh climate is not kind to crops, but some do grow and farmers experiment in expanding the harvest.
Opposite: this delightful mailbox mimics the style of a Nova Scotian clapboard house.
Pages 56–57: the Batoche National Historic Site on the banks of the South Saskatchewan River marks the site of the Northwest Rebellion of 1885. The church at the Metis Cemetery stands in prayer for those who gave their lives during the struggle.

Hector Lake in the Canadian Rockies was named for the British geologist, Sir James Hector. Nearby Kicking Horse Path was named for a horse that kicked Sir James.

From orchards to ice, from rainforest to ranchlands, British Columbia is known for its abundance of natural features and natural beauty. Here graceful aspen trees take their turn to impress.

Montréal's Olympic Stadium was built for the summer Olympic Games of 1976, and was quickly dubbed
'The Big O'. Locals changed that to 'The Big Owe', as the total debt of C$1 billion was only finally
paid off in the summer of 2006.
Opposite: as Montréal's Olympic Stadium rose in the 1970s, the new marina at Vancouver's Granville
Island was also under construction. Now hundreds of boats now bob, where previously dereliction and
rubbish once marred the mountain view.

On Cape Breton Island's northeast coast, the idyllic fishing village of Neil's Harbour lies just off the Cabot Trail. This lifeguard lookout watches out for when the waves start to flex their muscles. Opposite: the Pacific Rim National Park on Vancouver Island protects one of the most diverse areas in the country. The park has forests, beaches, islands, and almost 300 native archaeological sites. Pages 64–65: nature always has the power to transform the most familiar spots, and remind us again of their beauty. At Niagara Falls, the sunset paints the waters as they thunder over the edge.

This view is from Casa Loma, a fanciful private home that began life in 1911. The city skyline seems so permanent now that it is hard to imagine what this same view must have been when the house was new.

Baie-St-Paul sits where the Gouffre River flows into the mighty
St Lawrence. At a graveyard, a gilded angel is at peace with the view.
Pages 68–69: the Algonquin Provincial Park, the best-known in
Ontario, numbers thousands of lakes in among its forest-clad hills.
These canoeists know how this one, Smoke Lake, got its name.
Pages 72–73: in Vancouver's English Bay, Inukshuk stone creations
mark milestones or directions for the people of the Canadian Arctic.

Jasper National Park, on the western edge of Alberta, covers almost 4,200 square miles. Almost every one of these miles has a spectacular view to rival this, of Pyramid Lake.

Banff National Park was the first national park in Canada and was established in 1885. Since then, visitors have been able to stop and photograph the unchanging views like here at Bow Lake.

In fall the trees lining the Cabot Trail in the Cape Breton Islands National Park turn to yellows and oranges, to russets and golds. The area's rugged landscape and cool maritime climate allow a range of trees to grow.

Opposite: the barren rocks of Newfoundland's Tablelands come to life when the mountain streams start to flow. The unusual peroditite rocks found here lack the usual nutrients which enable plantlife to grow.

Pages 76–77: Bonaventure Island, off the tip of Quebec's Gaspé Peninsula, has the world's second-largest breeding colony of Northern Gannets.

Boats wait patiently, tied up to the pontoons in Vancouver's Coal Harbour. The harbor provides a vital link connecting downtown with Stanley Park, which in turn connects city to countryside.

Les Laurentides, to the north of Montréal, is a rural region of cottages, countryside, hearty food and a relaxing good time. This church in Saint-Adèle gives a flavor of the laid-back landscape.

The desolate Badlands of Alberta have been so described from the First Nations people onwards.
These sandstone sculptures, carved by the wind, are a rare feature in the barren landscape.
Opposite: visitors to the top of the CN Tower become spectators at Toronto's SkyDome stadium
when the retractable roof is open. The stadium is home to the city's football and baseball teams, and
is Toronto's largest indoor concert arena.

The Lobster Cove Head Lighthouse has lit the way for mariners since 1897. Although the light is now automated, the house remains open as a visitor center highlighting the way man has battled with and lived alongside the sea here for more than 4,000 years.

Opposite: the Northern Highlands of Nova Scotia's Cape Breton Island offer majestic scenery whether up in the hills or down by the shore, as here near the Cabot Trail between Neil's Harbour and Smelt Brook. It's a time to pause and look for whales in the bay.

Pages 84–85: Montréal's Biosphere on the Île Saint-Hélène was designed by, and originally named after, the architect Buckminster Fuller in 1967. Visitors still marvel at his design today.

Pages 88–89: Vancouver combines concrete high-rise buildings with waterside living, and modern commerce with a maritime heritage. It's no surprise that the city regularly comes near the top of lists of the world's best cities in which to live.

In the fishing villages of Nova Scotia the sea is an integral part of life. The implements which man has invented to battle the tides and haul in the fish are heroically simple.

Opposite: with five sails for a roof, Vancouver's Canada Place is a fitting building for a nation which knows what it's like to put out to sea to try to conquer the waves.

Pages 90–91: beneath the Eden-like Yukon landscape lay the gold that lured prospectors. In order to trade with Alaska, the Alaska Highway was built across its face. This beautiful and tranquil lake was created during construction of the highway.

The Abbey Chapel at St-Benoît-du-Lac in Quebec has a beautifully tranquil setting. The chapel welcomes the community's monks when they begin their day's prayers at 5am.

A rainbow links heaven and earth in the Yukon's remote Tombstone Mountains. The First Nations called them the Odhah Chaa Tat: 'among the sharp, ragged mountains'.